Meeting Jesus
on the Margins

MEDITATIONS ON MATTHEW 25

Bo Cox • Allison Duvall • Hugo Olaiz
Mike Kinman • Lee Anne Reat
Becca Stevens • Richelle Thompson

© 2015 Forward Movement

Forward Movement
412 Sycamore Street
Cincinnati, Ohio 45202-4195
800.543.1813
www.forwardmovement.org

ISBN 978-0-88028-414-1

Cover art: *Los Desaparecidos—The Missing Ones*, an acrylic on canvas painting by Jim apRoberts. View his work at www.jimaproberts.com.

Printed in the U.S.A.

Meeting Jesus
on the Margins

MEDITATIONS ON MATTHEW 25

Forward Movement
Cincinnati, Ohio

TABLE OF CONTENTS

T hen the king will say to those at his right hand, "Come, you that are blessed by my Father, inherit the kingdom prepared for you from the foundation of the world; for I was hungry and you gave me food, I was thirsty and you gave me something to drink, I was a stranger and you welcomed me, I was naked and you gave me clothing, I was sick and you took care of me, I was in prison and you visited me. Then the righteous will answer him, "Lord, when was it that we saw you hungry and gave you food, or thirsty and gave you something to drink? And when was it that we saw you a stranger and welcomed you, or naked and gave you clothing? And when was it that we saw you sick or in prison and visited you?" And the king will answer them, "Truly I tell you, just as you did it to one of the least of these who are members of my family, you did it to me."

—MATTHEW 25:34-40

CHAPTER 1

Meditations on Matthew 25

*For I was hungry
and you gave me food*

Ash Wednesday

Dear People of God: The first Christians observed with great devotion the days of our Lord's passion and resurrection, and it became the custom of the Church to prepare for them by a season of penitence and fasting. This season of Lent provided a time in which converts to the faith were prepared for Holy Baptism. It was also a time when those who, because of notorious sins, had been separated from the body of the faithful were reconciled by penitence and forgiveness, and restored to the fellowship of the Church. Thereby, the whole congregation was put in mind of the message of pardon and absolution set forth in the Gospel of our Savior, and of the need which all Christians continually have to renew their repentance and faith. —THE BOOK OF COMMON PRAYER, pp. 264-5

The simplest question is the most useful: Why?

We need always to be asking "Why?" and not letting our quickest answers, which are most deeply rooted in our prejudices, be our final answer.

When we see someone using the steps of a public library as a bed at night, we need to ask "Why?"

When we read a story about a transgender teenager committing suicide, we need to ask "Why?"

When we go into a grocery store in an impoverished neighborhood and see a fully stocked liquor shelf and no fresh produce, we need to ask "Why?"

When we learn we incarcerate a higher percentage of our citizens than any nation in the world, we need to ask "Why?"

When we see young people of color burn down the Quik Trip convenient store in Ferguson, Missouri, we need to ask "Why?"

And as we embark on our Lenten journey, we need to ask "Why?"

Our first answer, rooted in what we've always been taught, might be that we observe Lent as an exercise in self-flagellation, so that, in Paul's words, we might not "think of ourself more highly than we ought" (Romans 12:3). We might think our Lenten observance is grounded in our unworthiness. But we need to dig deeper.

The prayer at the beginning of our Ash Wednesday liturgy gives us the answer. We observe a holy Lent to remember Jesus' gospel of "pardon and absolution." Lent is not about confession and repentance as punishment but as a profound, grace-filled unburdening so that we might encounter the living Christ in all Christ's abundant joy.

This book sets our Lenten journey in that context of meeting Christ…meeting Christ right where he tells us he will be…in the hungry, the thirsty, the stranger, the naked, the sick, and the prisoner. It is a journey of seeing all those people as Jesus. Of asking "Why?" and not being satisfied by our first answer. Of realizing that those whom the world of power and privilege label as "them" are really the deepest and most sacred portion of "us."

—MIKE KINMAN

For I was hungry and you gave me food

In Fritz Eichenberg's 1953 wood engraving, *Christ of the Breadlines,* Jesus stands with six others who appear to be poor and perhaps homeless, huddled under blankets. Their heads are bowed. In prayer? In shame? In exhaustion? Jesus shares the despair and humiliation of the hungry waiting in long lines to receive their daily bread.

The fundamental lesson of Matthew 25 is that when we respond or fail to respond to the needs of others, we are responding or failing to respond to Christ. Salvation, in this passage, is a matter of how we treat "the least of these." Churches are very good at feeding people. Church folk are known for sumptuous potlucks and parties. We respond readily to calls for food at pantries that serve the poor, and many congregations serve dinners at shelters or in their own dining rooms to neighbors in need. We give generously to international organizations such as Episcopal Relief & Development when famine threatens whole populations.

But is that enough? We may be responding to only one aspect of the hunger that grips our sisters and brothers and ignoring our own hunger in the process. If we look closely at *Christ of the Breadlines,* we see more than hunger for food. Each person in the line is turned inward, alone and vulnerable. What we see goes beyond hunger for food. We see hunger for connection, hunger for relationship. Isn't that a hunger we all share, regardless of our economic circumstances?

When we recognize Christ's presence as we gather around tables with the poor, feeding programs transform into eucharistic celebrations, as hearts are filled along with stomachs. When we join in the meal we soon discover that we, too, are the hungry in need of food. We, too, are the lonely, afraid, and in need of friendship. We discover Christ in the other and Christ in ourselves.

—LEE ANNE REAT

FEBRUARY 12

They call it *la bestia*, which is Spanish for "the beast," and it runs from southern Mexico all the way to the US border. On a cargo train there is neither coach nor business class, but if you're foolish enough, or desperate enough, you might climb atop la bestia and, along with thousands of fellow freight hoppers, attempt the longest leg of your perilous journey to the US.

How dangerous that journey is! Men are often robbed or extorted. Women are sometimes raped or kidnapped. Along some sections of the trip, gangs may force you to pay $100 for the privilege of riding; if you refuse or cannot pay, you're thrown off the train.

Guatemalans, Salvadorans, and Hondurans ride la bestia to flee poverty and hunger. Ironically, the ride itself makes them poor and hungry.

Have you seen the YouTube clip? When la bestia approaches the town of Guadalupe in Veracruz, the migrant workers encounter a miracle: a small group of women, known as *las patronas*, standing by the railroad track with bags of food. If you're strong enough, you hold on for dear life with one hand and stretch the other out, as far as humanly possible, toward one of the patronas. And if you're lucky, you'll be able to catch a bag of rice or beans, a loaf of bread, or a bottle of water.

As the train passes at thirty miles an hour, the patronas do not ask questions. They simply give away the food.

"Adiós, abuelita," call some of the riders as they catch the only decent meal they'll have on that train. "Adiós, my child," replies seventy-five-year-old Leonila Vázquez. "God bless you."

—HUGO OLAIZ

FEBRUARY 13

Pipes frozen again, windchill below zero, my Lenten journey begins in the bitter cold of winter. Spaghetti night is postponed until the pipes thaw out again, so soup it shall be…tomato soup that reminds me of the bounty of late summer.

Shelves in our garage hold a rainbow of mason jars full of bright yellow, orange, red, and purple tomatoes from the summer harvest. I pick diced yellow heirlooms and plump whole Romas. With some aromatics—sautéed garlic and caramelized onions—this meal will be simple, yet nourishing.

The wind squeals as it tears past my kitchen window. In the pale yellow light of the street lamp, I see neighbor boys pulling their jackets close to their bodies, hurrying home, pushed faster by the blowing snow. A solitary figure trudges the opposite way, headlong into the snow. His body (thankfully) appears well-layered against the storm. He pushes an unwieldy shopping cart over the icy ground, back wheels whipping side to side. Amidst the cans and bottles in the cart are some trash bags. A blanket is tucked in the childseat. I watch him walk past the house until he's out of view. I wonder where he's headed. The Family Dollar Store is just down the street, several day centers for the homeless within a few blocks. I return to stirring the pot on the stovetop, add the tomatoes, broth, and some spices to the pot. I say a prayer. I feel a sadness creeping and settling in my stomach, along with embarrassment at how I had felt just moments before: complaining of frozen pipes and cranky about streams of cold air breaking through cracks under our front door. All the while I am at my warm stove, stirring a colorful, bubbling pot. The lonely figure outside my window, pushing his argumentative cart, leaves me standing convicted.

This Lent begins with a recognition of my privilege and my blessings. I often give up something during Lent, deny myself something from my abundance. Perhaps this Lent I will not give up but instead give away. I can give away my time, giving of my energies to assist a neighbor, an agency, or a ministry. I can give away from my abundance, offering ingredients and time to provide soup at a community meal, or offering the warmth of a winter coat from my closet.

Perhaps, by giving away instead of giving up, I will discover a greater abundance, the paradox of our faith.

—ALLISON DUVALL

A feast without a fast is gluttony. So each year the church community sets aside a season of fasting for all people to remember what it means to know hunger and to long for a feast. Hunger is one of the gifts of Lent. Hunger can carve compassion onto hearts, close up the space between myths and facts in social justice, and clear foggy, sated minds.

To be hungry in a Lenten sense is to remember that the pronouncement by Jesus that the poor will always be with us is a blessing, not a curse. It's a blessing to remember our poverty and hunger and to remember how we have been fed. A church without beggars is a museum. So it is that as beggars we bless the church with our presence. All people who attend church services are beggars, holding out hands for a bit of bread as we are reminded of our hunger. Thank God we know our hunger and where to turn for food. Fasting is a reminder that hunger is not just a theology though; it is a real physical pain and a longing to be fed.

Fasting is a spiritual discipline carved out of abundance. When someone decides to fast, it is a preparation of their body, mind, and spirit for renewal, penitence, or healing. It is the connection between the haves and have-nots, even though fasting itself is just a small taste of hunger.

Matthew 25 teaches that Christ is in the hunger, and Christ is in the morsel of bread offered at altars. May this season allow you to know both the gift of hunger and the gift of being fed.

God forgive us our gluttony and unsated appetites. Forgive us our need to fill ourselves with things that never stop the hunger. Thank you for the gift of fasting. Teach us to tune our ears to hear the cry of those around us who are hungry, thirsty, naked, suffering, and dying, so that in serving one another in need, we find ourselves beside you. Amen.

—Becca Stevens

Most of us have never been hungry, really hungry. Oh sure, we've felt hunger pangs an hour or so before sitting down to a big meal, but we've never been hungry enough to dig through garbage cans for our next meal. Food insecurity means having limited or uncertain access to adequate food, i.e. not always knowing where your next meal will come from.

There are plenty of social and economic causes of food insecurity. One cause that is receiving increased attention is the existence of "food deserts"—areas in which low-income individuals must travel more than one mile to a grocery store that carries a full range of foods, including fresh fruits and vegetables. Those of us with cars don't think twice about bringing home several bags of nutritious foods, a gallon of milk, and food for our pets. But can you imagine carrying that much on a bus or bicycle? And food pantries in low-income communities are usually not equipped to provide fresh foods on a consistent basis.

So what can we do? "Give a man a fish and he eats for a day; teach a man to fish and he eats for a lifetime." It seems that more and more, this old Chinese proverb is being practiced. The indignity inherent in standing in line at a food pantry is being replaced by the pride of growing one's own food. Community gardens are popping up all over urban and suburban landscapes. Children and adults are learning to plant and harvest their own foods. Workshops are teaching people how to cook with unfamiliar vegetables and herbs. Some communities have even opened mobile grocery stores that take fresh foods directly into underserved neighborhoods.

Jesus' call to feed the hungry goes well beyond direct distribution of food to the poor. Feeding the hungry extends to teaching and working alongside others, to pressuring grocery store chains to locate in underserved areas, and to creating jobs that support families in climbing out of poverty. How can we help feed our hungry neighbors?

—LEE ANNE REAT

Out of a total population of 7.2 billion, 805 millon people in the world do not have enough food to lead an active, healthy life. One out of every nine people in the world go to bed hungry every night.

Somehow, you and I manage to find ways to detach from the reality that we, together with three of our closest friends, are responsible for the life of one other person—responsible in the sense that it is within our power to change their life.

Looking at the face of a young man panhandling at an intersection, my dog Hope (cruelly ironic in this situation) barks, and the man smiles at her. He nods a look of understanding to me, like it's okay to enjoy living in this world where I can afford a car and a dog, and where he's reduced to shuffling up and down the street with his one stiff leg, asking for handouts. It's even okay if I wonder if that limp is real or a manufactured prop to elicit pity. It's okay, he nods, and his eyes really mean it.

Of course, as I pull away, heading on to the dog-training class, I contemplate my blessing from this beggar. Why? Why was he so forgiving of Hope's bark and my freedom from the responsibility of helping him?

Long before the world had this many people in it, Jesus knew that our basic nature would be to look out for ourselves first and that our preoccupation with self would do just what it did in his day: produce a world where some people have more than enough and some don't. Jesus also knew that the key to the kingdom of heaven could be found in the moments when we simply slowed down long enough to look into the eye of someone in need and saw him.

—**Bo Cox**

FEBRUARY 17

I'm not sure whether I attend a church with a food bank attached to it, or a food bank with a church attached to it.

Every Sunday, after Holy Eucharist, we walk downstairs and find ourselves in a crowded room with people waiting to be fed. Twenty, thirty, forty people waiting to get a number, and then waiting for their number to be called, so that they can go into our pantry and get some groceries. Dorothy oversees this controlled chaos.

In the meantime, Mark rolls up the kitchen window and announces that lunch is ready. Every Saturday he spends hours cooking these meals. We all form a line to get something to eat.

Sometimes I can smell the alcohol on someone's breath. But I don't think Jesus would care, and neither should I.

Some of these folks seem standoffish, aloof, even rude. But I don't think Jesus would care, and neither should I.

Sometimes a person smells of tobacco, body odor, even urine. But I don't think Jesus would care, and neither should I.

Aren't the free lunches and food bank an extension of our eucharist? Aren't Mark and Dorothy and I and the standoffish man in the red T-shirt all part of the same broken Body of Christ?

I'm not sure whether I attend a church with a food bank attached to it, or a food bank with a church attached to it. But I don't think Jesus would care. And neither should I.

—Hugo Olaiz

Meeting Jesus on the Margins

Monday morning, the children bounced and twittered as they stood in line for breakfast. Eyes bigger than their stomachs, they piled pancakes and sausage patties on their trays. Despite the camp staff's attempts to encourage them to be more moderate with their food choices, by the end of breakfast, the trash bin was filled to overflowing with food. The children spent the morning in learning centers, the prime focus of Reading Camp, a literacy ministry in the Diocese of Lexington. Rotating through six focus areas, the children worked in small groups with teachers to strengthen their skills.

For low-income and underachieving students, summer is a devastating time. Whereas more affluent peers benefit from educational summer enrichment programs, these children fall prey to summer learning loss. Reading Camp's mission is to stem the tide of summer learning loss and to enrich and improve students' reading skills, building a stronger foundation on which to begin the next school year.

After the learning center rotations finished, the teenage counselors met the campers and trekked back to the dining hall. One little boy seemed particularly bewildered. "What are we doing?" he asked the counselor and teacher standing with him. "We're lining up for lunch," the counselor responded. "But… we've already eaten today!" The counselor and teacher looked at each other in surprise. All of a sudden, they realized that breakfast had not simply been about children with eyes larger than their stomachs. The children believed that this was the only meal they would get, so they had better eat up.

It was a tangible encounter with what affluent Americans experience as a statistic: in the 2013-2014 school year, 70 percent of the five billion meals served to public school students were free or reduced price. In the summers, those same children survive on only one or two meals per day.

The all-volunteer Reading Camp staff, from parishes across the diocese, sat with this story and this experience, processing it together for the remainder of the week. For many, this was their first real encounter with poverty. We left that week of Reading Camp—a week of domestic mission engagement—transformed. We began to understand data in a new way: behind each statistic is a story, a person, and a deep hunger.

—**ALLISON DUVALL**

CHAPTER 2

Meditations on Matthew 25

*I was thirsty and you gave me
something to drink*

Imagine the state of the world in which Jesus lived, where giving drink to the thirsty made his top six list of important things to do. Reconstruct in your mind the circumstances in which being able to drink the most basic life-sustaining liquid is problematic. In the arid lands of the Middle East, access to water was a matter of life and death.

Settlements were established near available water or where wells could be dug. When those traveling from place to place approached a village or an oasis, they depended on the hospitality of strangers. Dry and thirsty travelers counted on a strict code of conduct. In these circumstances, drink was given to the thirsty, not so much as an optional act of personal charity but as the fulfillment of a widely understood obligation: those who had water gave it to those in need.

It was understood across the region that no one who owned or controlled those resources should exercise stewardship over them in a way that would deprive others of life-sustaining goods. This moral obligation was imbedded in the fabric of these communities through binding customs. We're not talking about the generosity between one person who has water and another who does not. The heart of the matter was justice. It's a community that creates codes and structures in a world in which the resources required for human flourishing are denied to too many people, while others have more than they need.

Imagine creating a society in which everyone is always expected to give drink to the thirsty. Imagine social standards that called on everyone, time after time, to give of their abundance to those in need. Imagine establishing a habit of giving that reflects gratitude for what each of us has been given and developing an understanding of responsible stewardship that governs the way we live in community.

—Becca Stevens

As they settled into the pew, I began the spiel. I introduced myself and welcomed them to the church. I asked whether they had ever attended an Episcopal church before. When they said no, I launched into spiel, part 2. I explained that during Holy Eucharist, all baptized Christians were welcome to receive. I told them the options for intinction or common cup, how the congregation typically files to the altar rail and kneels. And I explained they could receive a blessing if they didn't want to take communion. Then I asked if they had any questions.

"Um, yes," the wife murmured. "What's a eucharist?"

I had skipped right over the heart of the service and into the mechanics. It was like offering Manola Blahnik high heels to the barefoot. Or sparkling San Pellegrino water to the thirsty. If folks don't know about the body and bread of Christ—about this sacred meal that connects us to Christ then, now, and always—then they probably don't care (or understand) instructions about whether to dip or sip.

Most people in my social circle are church-going Christians. And if they don't attend church now, they used to, or are at least familiar with the traditions. But I too often forget that one in five Americans are, as the Pew Research Center states, "religiously unaffiliated." More and more people are growing up without ever attending church. The parables of Jesus aren't rich examples of grace and love but social media memes and movie quotes. After all, I wonder how many know that Spiderman's Uncle Ben was paraphrasing the Gospel of Luke when he cautioned his nephew, "With great power comes great responsibility."

The spiritual-but-not-religious, the "nones," the religiously unaffiliated are searching for meaning in their lives. They are thirsty, and Jesus is asking us to share the living water.

—Richelle Thompson

Several years ago a young man participating in a wilderness survival adventure died of thirst. He was just 100 yards from a pool of fresh water when he dropped dead. Instructors and other participants watched, never offering him a drink of the emergency water they were carrying. When asked why they did not help him, instructors said they wanted him to succeed in reaching the goal he had set for himself.

Our Lenten journey begins with Jesus in the wilderness, where, Mark tells us, he was attended by angels. How thirsty he must have been! How thankful for the water provided by angels during those forty days.

Thirst is one of the body's early warning systems. It signals that one's internal fluids are out of balance, a balance that is essential for the body to function properly. Too little water leads to light-headedness, muscle cramps, and confusion. Too much water can have the same symptoms and lead to liver and kidney problems and congestive heart failure. A severe fluid imbalance in the body can result in death.

As humans we thirst for many things, not just water. During Lent we venture with Jesus into the dryness of the desert. Our hearts thirst for closeness to God. We are aware of an imbalance in our relationship with the divine. We search for springs of living water.

Matthew 25 is a call to give care, but it can also be a call to accept the care offered to us. In our social and economic privilege, we often wince at the prospect of asking for help. Like the young man on the survival course, we focus on reaching some arbitrary goal of our own imagining and ignore our need for help. Spiritual journeys are every bit as fraught with danger as hikes in the wilderness. We had best go with companions, spiritual friends who will answer our pleas for water when we thirst, hope when we despair, a healing touch when we experience pain. We must learn to ask for help when we need it and accept help when it is offered. Our salvation depends on it.

—LEE ANNE REAT

I moved to northern California in 1992, the year a drought ended. That winter, the snow covered all the mountains of the Sierra Nevada. In the spring, the snow melted and watered the trees and the wildflowers of those mountains. There were many trees and many wildflowers, yet they did not consume all the water.

There were all kinds of animals in those mountains: rabbits and bears, snakes and raccoons, squirrels and deer. There were also many birds. They all drank from the water that rolled down the streams.

The streams eventually merge to form the American River. I have seen young people there, swimming and floating in boats and inner tubes. They laughed and hooted as they came down the rapids.

The river flows into the San Francisco Bay and eventually into the Pacific, where all kinds of marine life thrive. I know this because I have swam there. And sometimes I would go to Point Reyes, where I could see the white jets of gray whales migrating 10,000 miles between Alaska and Baja California. It was a sight that filled me with awe. The whales were huge, yet they did not consume all the water either.

Biologists would call this an ecosystem, but I call it an act of sharing. Then the water evaporates, becoming clouds, and the process begins all over again.

Today I heard on the radio that drought has returned to California. There is fear that people may consume all the water.

—Hugo Olaiz

Sometimes beginning to see through the eyes of another starts with recognizing that you have enough. Seeing your own circumstances in a new light, you learn to inhabit a posture of gratitude.

In my experience, the tradition of giving up for Lent has always come from a place of comfortable middle-class plenitude. I give up dessert because I enjoy too much of it. I give up eating out because I can so readily and easily do it. I give up meat because I eat it with such regularity. But I've never restricted my use of water. Rarely have I stopped to consider the overwhelming privilege of turning on the tap with the constant expectation that water will flow from it. I've never considered the possibility that the water won't come when I want it.

This is a privilege, a privilege of geography, wealth, education, class, and history. Fulfilled expectations are my privilege.

It is also a privilege that I am not often challenged to consider that my fulfilled expectations might mean that someone else's expectations are dashed. Because of privilege I don't consider that leaving the water running while brushing my teeth or caring for a manicured lawn means that those precious liquid resources are not being used elsewhere.

If access to water is a human right, then it is my human responsibility to develop a mindfulness and thoughtfulness toward how I use this water. The water of life in Christ is not mine and mine alone but is a gift and a grace freely given to the world. So too is the water of life not mine and mine alone to use carelessly and gratuitously.

It is my Christian responsibility to develop an awareness for the impact my behavior has on others.

Perhaps this Lent will be less a time of self-deprivation and more a time of prayerfully and thoughtfully developing an awareness of how I use the precious resources around me.

—ALLISON DUVALL

Bingo is the most popular activity we do at the psych hospital. It is not unusual to find that by the time the whirlwind of a mental health episode has subsided, folks find themselves without—without homes, without friends, without jobs, without belonging. In light of this, it is understandable why seemingly small items are valued so much.

That's part of the reason bingo is so popular. Soft drinks are the most coveted of treats, and every time we play bingo you hear someone say they're going to die if they don't win a soda.

One particular time a man began to worry me. From the minute people entered the lobby, he was vocal about his desire to have a soda and his "need" hadn't quieted throughout the evening. When others won, he yelled across the room.

"I better win!" At first he said it like he was joking, but as he grew more frustrated, it took on the tone of a threat and it wasn't long before worried looks passed. Would he follow through on his threats? Would staff members be able to keep him from hurting someone?

I usually call the numbers, and although I fight the urge to play God and manipulate the outcomes, I was tempted to let him win just so we could avoid a possible catastrophe. But I didn't have to—just then he won.

"Yes!" he exclaimed. Clad in yellow hospital pajamas, he strode up to the table to present his card, looking around proudly and grinning widely. I read the numbers off and, sure enough, he had won. He claimed his prize and held it up for the whole room to see. I just knew he'd twist off the top and guzzle it down right there.

So when he walked back to his table and passed it around, sharing the soda with the people around him, I knew I was witnessing a holy moment.

—**Bo Cox**

The mountains whisper a siren song.

Past Georgian-style county courthouses and dollar stores, house trailers with sagging front porches and long-eared dogs. Through the one-lane underpass that shakes when the trains head west from the coal mines.

Up and around roads chiseled into rock, and finally to the mountaintop where cell phones don't work and time passes at its own pace. These 800 acres next to the Daniel Boone National Forest offer rest to the weary and refreshment to all.

The cathedral at the top of the mountain is a rare sight. Made from timbers on the land, it is built in Gothic style, wooden trusses seventy feet high. A wall of windows overlooks the mountain, images so beautiful with colors so bold, so deep, a tapestry beyond any fabricated stained glass.

The orientation of the building was determined in medieval fashion. The bishop and a few others spent the night on the mountain on the eve of Saint George's Day. When the sun rose through the mist, the bishop marked the exact spot with his pastoral staff, and the cathedral was built on that axis.

Six decades later, prayers are offered from that altar, with sunlight entering the cathedral inch by inch.

Children and grandparents, families and teens climb the rocks, shiver in the Bat Cave, swim in the cool water, give snakes wide berth, read on cabin porches, play tag in the basin, sing around the campfire.

A popular hike is to the spring, where crystal water flows. A ladle stays nearby, so all who come may slake their thirst and drink from the mountain.

—RICHELLE THOMPSON

CHAPTER 3

Meditations on Matthew 25

*I was a stranger
and you welcomed me*

"My name is not 'refugee.'" She spoke with confidence, with certainty.

"My name is not 'refugee,'" she said. "Call me by my name. My name is Grace."

We sat in the airy and bright atrium of a hotel, engaged in an interview that started mildly but soon became a tour de force. A declaration. A stand. My colleague, the communications manager for Episcopal Migration Ministries, and I stood convicted. This vibrant, strong young woman, in one deft and powerful phrase, shifted our thinking, our approach, our language.

Language matters, this young woman was saying. She was uniquely qualified to know this, fluent as she was in a half dozen languages—not uncommon for many refugees. Language matters a great deal. We live into what we say. Words are self-fulfilling prophecies. When we call a person "refugee," we attach layers and categories to the word and the person. We assign vulnerability and not strength, needs and not resources, weakness and not agency.

When we call someone "stranger," we "other" them. When we call someone "refugee" or "immigrant," we forget that we too were strangers in the land of Egypt. That Jesus, our Lord and God, when he was but a child, lived as a refugee too.

When next you find yourself inclined to see someone you don't know as stranger, take a moment's pause. Perhaps wave in greeting. Perhaps say hello and ask, "How are you?" A small bit of kindness, a small gesture of welcome, may go a long way—not only for the person you greet but for your own soul. You may, in fact, begin to find your understanding of neighbor shifting and growing. You may begin to see and find God in places you did not look before.

—**Allison Duvall**

What is a stranger? When I ask myself that question, one of the answers I come up with is that a stranger is someone I have difficulty looking in the eye and/or acknowledging their space and/or existence. Why?

Is it because I, in my own self-deluded and self-imposed importance, don't have the time to get to know them, or just that I don't care?

If I don't care, is it because there's nothing they can do for me? Because, trust me, there are people I do care about and, whether or not I want to admit it, one of their common markers is that they bring something to the table, at least as far as I am concerned.

But Jesus says we should care for and welcome those strangers even if—maybe especially if—there's nothing they can do for us, even if they bring nothing to the table.

So I have to ask myself: if Jesus didn't have anything to offer me, would I still believe in him? Would I still try to follow his example? If I got nothing out of believing in Jesus, would I still believe?

An entire religion is named after this Jesus, and plenty of folks say they care about him, but what I find in too many conversations is that this care, love, and concern is rooted in what Jesus can do for them. Too often, Christianity becomes not "Do I believe in Jesus?" or "Do I try to follow Jesus' example?" but rather, "What do I believe about Jesus?" and suddenly it's about belonging to an exclusive country club where everyone looks and believes like I do. Oh, and by the way, if you don't belong, you're doomed. In those settings, if you look around, there are no strangers.

Lest we forget, Jesus turned the religious establishment of his day on its ear with his radical inclusiveness. Are we really followers of his if we fail to follow that example?

What if this was the acid test of Christianity: "How many strangers have you welcomed today?"

—Bo Cox

There are a lot of numbers to remember when you walk in downtown Salt Lake City. That's because most of the street names are numbers. On 200 South, for example, you'll find one of the finest restaurants in town—and one of the most beautiful.

The restaurant seats 160. The focal point is its exhibition kitchen, where the chef and his assistants create stunning dishes—or so I'm told.

It's not cheap to dine there. An entrée will cost you between $30 and $50. Go with a date, add appetizers and drinks, and you'll easily end up spending $200. With those prices, I've seen this restaurant many times but only through the windows.

The windows themselves are a work of art: fourteen of them, two stories tall, each topped by a Roman arch, and each arch topped by a mythological head in relief. On sunny days the restaurant is bathed in sunlight—even the rooms for private parties— because the French doors let the light through.

There's one more thing about the windows. Each windowsill has an iron rail, and each rail is lined with exactly thirty-five spikes. No one homeless could sit or try to sleep on those thick sills. No panhandler could ruin the view of the dining customers or block the sunlight.

There are a lot of numbers to remember about this restaurant: 160 seats, 14 huge windows, and 35 spikes along each window—490 spikes in total, each of them pointing toward heaven.

—HUGO OLAIZ

The gatekeeper opens the gate for him, and the sheep hear his voice. He calls his own sheep by name and leads them out. When he has brought out all his own, he goes ahead of them, and the sheep follow him because they know his voice. They will not follow a stranger, but they will run from him because they do not know the voice of strangers.—John 10:3-5

The closest thing to the realm of God I have ever experienced is the Magdalene community begun in Nashville, Tennessee, by Becca Stevens. Women who have endured lives of prostitution, violence, and abuse find a sisterhood of recovery that takes them from the deepest poverty to the richest abundance of life.

The women of Magdalene are my spiritual guides. And they have names—names like Shana and Shelia and Katrina and Ronza and Melody and Melanie. When they see me, they call me by name, and when I see them, I call them by name.

The sisterhood of Magdalene is not just a two-year residential recovery program. It is a promise of hope rooted in the principle that each woman is not a statistic but a whole person with a sacred name, a sacred face, a sacred story.

As long as we are trying to end homelessness without attaching faces and names, we will never end homelessness.

As long as we are trying to end poverty and don't make it personal, we will never end poverty.

As long as we are trying to end hunger and refuse to meet hungry people face to face, we will never end hunger.

Because we will never care enough, unless we see ourselves—unless we see Jesus' face on the faces of the people who are suffering.

As long as we view the deep brokennesses of our world as "problems" and the people as statistics, we will never care enough to get the job done.

Jesus gives us the model of the Good Shepherd—and the Good Shepherd calls each of the sheep *by name*. That's our model. Our hearts are not strangely warmed by statistics, but we are moved by images of God with names.

The deep truth behind welcoming the stranger is that the very act of welcoming makes the person not a stranger. And the first act of welcoming is the most powerful—sharing names. When we share names, we become human to each other. And that is the beginning of activating the healing power of love.

—MIKE KINMAN

MARCH 1

When we see a homeless or hungry person, a stranger in need, instead of saying, "There but for the grace of God go I," maybe we could say, "There goes God." This reminds us of the truth that in loving our neighbors, we are meeting God. The heart of the matter is that God is in every person and every person should be treated accordingly: with love and respect.

The story of how strangers feel when they are recognized as brothers and sisters is inspiring. One woman I worked with at Thistle Farms, a community of women survivors, wrote:

> I used to get high under the walking bridge near downtown. I would get high and pray and listen to the birds. I really think the birds kept me going. One day I was sitting there, crazy as hell. I hadn't had a bath, hadn't eaten. I had a knife and was contemplating suicide when a man named Roy came and sat down beside me. He asked what I was doing. I told him I was tired and ready to give up. He invited me to go with him to a place called Mt. Neboh Church. So I went. When I got there they gave me clothes, let me take a bath, and fed me. Right after church several people were going to do an outreach on the streets. They invited me to come along. The women from the church were giving bags of toiletries and snacks away to women walking the streets. I saw them treat the stranger, me, with love. They were partnering with a community called Magdalene, and

they invited me to come and live. The problem was I couldn't stay clean. It would take me almost another year to give up the drugs, but I am so thankful that God didn't give up on me.

She reminds all of us that the heart of church work is seeing the stranger as God and seeking out the lost sheep. The strangers who have become witnesses to how love heals lie at the heart of the gospel.

—Becca Stevens

March 2

As a teenager, I discovered something about the nature of God: I found God and God found me in those places I least expected, in those places where I was most uncomfortable, in the unfamiliar, out-of-the-ordinary, outside-of-my-comfort zones. I found God on Sunday morning sometimes, in the mystery and power of Holy Eucharist, in the enchanting music of the choir and organ, in the solemnity of our common prayer. But for a good part of my childhood, the church space was filled with similitude, homogeneity, and the normal. It wasn't until I was outside of the normal and mundane that God *really* found me, in an arresting, powerful way.

My first experience of pushing outside of the familiar, into the unknown, was at age fifteen, volunteering with a diocesan ministry called Reading Camp. It was the first time in my life that I met children whose lives were so different from my own. Some ate only one meal a day in the summers. Others had blistered toes and bloodied heels from the friction caused by their only pair of too-small shoes. And then there was the literacy instruction—the foundation of the entire ministry, offered in an encouraging, positive, loving environment. The children blossomed with the individual attention and supportive instruction. At night, adult staff members visited the children's cabins to read a bedtime story. The majority of campers remarked on how much they loved the bedtime story. No one had ever read a bedtime story to them before.

Powerful things happened in my soul during that one week of camp. Part of the transformation was seeing my own life in stark relief to lives so different from my own—recognizing my own privilege in a way I never had before. The other part of the transformation was the table-turning power of relationship—the way my insides were spilled out, shaken up, and put back together in a new way. There's something about following Jesus that does that—we are broken open and made a new creation—over and over again.

—ALLISON DUVALL

MARCH 3

Mike Brown and I lived seven miles apart for his entire life…but it might as well have been 700…or 7,000.

I hope we won't have forgotten by the time you are reading this but Mike Brown was the nineteen-year-old African American young man killed by Ferguson police officer Darren Wilson on August 9, 2014. His death was the spark that ignited the new civil rights movement in this country.

I spent many nights during the fall of 2014 standing with protesters, chanting Mike Brown's name. But Mike Brown was a stranger to me. And that was part of the problem.

Mike Brown was a stranger to me not because we live in a big city and you can't possibly know everyone, but because I am white, and Mike Brown lived and died in an area of St. Louis where I rarely went. I knew only a handful of people who lived in Ferguson, and I never spent my money there.

Mike Brown was a stranger to me because as a white person in St. Louis, I pretty much stayed in the white areas of St. Louis, and those are areas where he was not welcome.

Mike Brown was a stranger to me because as a white person, I was comfortable living in my privilege. I was comfortable not considering who he might be and what his life might be like.

Mike Brown was a stranger to me because I ignored Jesus' gospel imperative to go into those places where strangers live and to meet Jesus there.

Our nation's original sin of racism lives on in our deep segregations between race and class. We are strangers to one another. And it is incumbent upon those of us with power and privilege in our society to hear Matthew 25 and take it to heart. It is incumbent upon us to welcome the stranger where we live and to be pilgrims to places we might not normally choose to go, and learn names, and build relationships and not so much bring Jesus there but recognize that Jesus is already there, waiting to be met.

—Mike Kinman

MARCH 4

It is a sad fact that churches feel the need to post signs ALL ARE WELCOME. Why should we need to advertise that fact?

Jesus lived his entire ministry among strangers—people outside the dominant social and religious norms of his day. He spent his time with all the wrong people—sinners, tax collectors, lepers, women, smelly fishermen and shepherds, and foreigners. Yet even the disciples had to ask, "When was it that we saw you a stranger and welcomed you?"

If we are honest with ourselves, the church has been, and remains in some cases, one of the least welcoming places we inhabit. The saying has long been true that the most segregated hour of the week is Sunday morning. Our signs say ALL ARE WELCOME, but our behavior often says STRANGER DANGER.

"Not us," you say. "See our sign!" But there are a lot of "ifs" associated with being fully accepted into church communities. You are welcome *if* you are the right color, *if* you speak the right language, *if* you wear the right clothing and smell good, *if* you love the same people we love. These ifs are so deeply ingrained in our various cultures that we may be largely unaware that we communicate them. But the stranger notices our discomfort— diverted eyes, purses tucked closer to the body, impenetrable circles of conversation at coffee hour.

It is difficult and often painful work to be radically honest with ourselves, to see that our actions do not always match our intent. Signs that say ALL ARE WELCOME are a good first step in welcoming the stranger. Our behaviors will change as we take time to think and pray about how we do and do not welcome strangers into our lives, at church, and in other settings.

How can we face the limits of our experience and understanding in ways that challenge our fears and transform our world views? How can we practice the radical welcome Jesus teaches us?

—LEE ANNE REAT

MARCH 5

They came to Jericho. As he and his disciples and a large crowd were leaving Jericho, Bartimaeus son of Timaeus, a blind beggar, was sitting by the roadside. When he heard that it was Jesus of Nazareth, he began to shout out and say, "Jesus, Son of David, have mercy on me!" Many sternly ordered him to be quiet, but he cried out even more loudly, "Son of David, have mercy on me!" Jesus stood still and said, "Call him here." And they called the blind man, saying to him, "Take heart; get up, he is calling you." So throwing off his cloak, he sprang up and came to Jesus. Then Jesus said to him, "What do you want me to do for you?" The blind man said to him, "My teacher, let me see again." Jesus said to him, "Go; your faith has made you well." Immediately he regained his sight and followed him on the way. —Mark 10:46-52*

In her book, *Radical Welcome,* the Rev. Stephanie Spellers talks about three types of welcome that strangers can experience when they come into our churches:

Inviting—"You are welcome to come in and be just like the rest of us."

Inclusion—"You are welcome to come in and be yourself, but off on the margins where you will never influence our dominant culture."

Radical Welcome—"You are welcome to come in and be yourself, and we will be changed by you."

Our model in Christ is radical welcome. The Bartimaeus story is Jesus showing us how to welcome the stranger. Over his disciples' objections, Jesus brings Bartimaeus right into the center of the community, removes all the barriers between Bartimaeus and the community, and at the end Bartimaeus is "one of them"…and the disciples are changed (we hope) by the experience.

In Matthew 25, Jesus tells us the stranger *is* him. That means any other welcome but radical welcome is idolatry—either through demanding Christ be in our own image or intentionally keeping Christ out of the center of our lives.

What kind of welcome do you practice?

—MIKE KINMAN

CHAPTER 4

Meditations on Matthew 25

*I was naked and you
gave me clothing*

Since I was a young child, I have been a student of dance. Today I continue my study of the art form as a teacher (truly the most intensive way to be a student). In such a visual and expressive form, costume matters a great deal. Costume sets the audience's expectations and creates parameters around the narrative being portrayed. In my particular world of Irish dance, costume further informs the dancer's self-perception. Dancers typically own one and only one costume. The color and shape, design and fabric adorn the dancer and make her feel powerful, graceful, dramatic, elegant, and in control. As over the top as such costumes can be, they seem to connect us to some primal tendencies; like packrats or magpies, we are attracted to the shiny, the glittery, the extravagant, and the unique. And we feel a certain way about ourselves when we adorn our physical selves in this way.

In much the same way, the philosophies, outlooks, paradigms, aspirations, and prayers that we choose to adorn our minds and our hearts each day affect how we think and feel about ourselves and others. There's very little that we can control in the world around us: we cannot control the outcome of a significant meeting; we cannot dictate another person's contribution to our conversation; we cannot shift entire systems alone, cannot save a person or institution, cannot force external change. But we can sculpt, mold, and nourish our internal presence, our approach to the art of living. We can choose calm over anxiety, patience over haste, presence over disconnection. We can clothe ourselves with blessing through the practices of our faith tradition. And we can be a blessing to others.

From nakedness, from a blank slate, how will we clothe ourselves? Will we clothe ourselves with compassion, gentleness, and self care? Will we clothe ourselves in the knowledge and love of God so that we might share God's peace with others?

When you have been adorned in self-doubt, insult, or injury, return to the still middle point. Return to nakedness, to quiet, to calm, to peace, to a judgment-free and value-free place. Remember that you are beloved, you are worthy. Clothe yourself; share with others this knowledge.

—ALLISON DUVALL

March 7

The first sign of falling from grace in the story of Adam and Eve was their feeling of nakedness. In that context, being naked is more than not having clothes on; it is feeling shame, being exposed and vulnerable. In Matthew 25, Jesus says that when we are naked and someone offers clothing, it is a great gift. In the larger sense, it means we are offered grace, security, and a means to move freely in this world.

For twenty years I have tended the community of Thistle Farms, residences and a bath-and-body care company for survivors of sexual trafficking. I do not think there is a community more naked and exposed in this world. To offer this community clothing means we need to offer a path to economic freedom, access to health care and dentists, advocates in court, and sanctuary where it is safe to sleep. It takes a broken community to remind people they are naked. It takes a loving community to help clothe those same folks.

I remember the time when a woman who had come from Central America moved into one of our residential homes and was given clothing. A week later another woman came from prison and roomed with her. The newest resident was supposed to appear in court the next morning. When she woke up, the woman who had been there a week had laid out one of her outfits (the fanciest one!) so the new woman could go to court dressed well. The woman who had been there a week had only three or four outfits, but she knew what it was like to be naked and gratefully gave up her new and finest clothes. The woman went to court dressed—with gratitude, with confidence, and with a loving community behind her that would never let her feel naked again. To be clothed by a loving community dresses us in grace and mercy. Those are gifts that cannot be stripped away.

—BECCA STEVENS

MARCH 8

In 2008, a group of women from a neighborhood of Buenos Aires, Argentina, started to get together once a week to knit. They knitted squares of 8-by-8 inches, then stitched the squares together to create woolen blankets. Once they had finished a few blankets, they sent them to needy families living in remote parts of Argentina.

The women started small—and without a penny. Once, in order to raise funds, they decided to use wool left over from other projects to knit a multicolored scarf. Then they organized a raffle with the scarf as the prize; with the money raised from the raffle, they purchased their next supply of wool.

Made always in *punto Santa Clara* (garter stitch), the blankets have beautiful designs evocative of American quilts. The women named their group *Abrigarte* (Spanish for "To Keep You Warm").

Over the last few years, the group has grown. A pool of women regularly donate wool or knit squares from their homes. Volunteers, sometimes from other nonprofits, help to identify needy areas and transport the blankets. And now the group knits other articles that people need, such as scarves, hats, ponchos, and baby booties.

These women's busy hands are God's hands, and their hearts are God's heart. Through their labor of love, God keeps thousands of men, women, and children warm during Argentina's harsh winters.

—Hugo Olaiz

MARCH 9

He smelled.

I tried the subtle scoot down the pew, but it was a crowded evening service. The tongue of his boots lolled to the side, his laces untied and tattered. He wore several layers of clothes; like a lot of homeless folks, he carried his entire wardrobe on his back. Dirt etched the lines of his knuckles, and his fingernails were torn and ragged.

The service honored our retiring bishop, and most, including me, were dressed to the nines. The presiding bishop was preaching, the choirs singing, and this man nodded off to sleep. I've always thought churches should leave their doors unlocked and the pews open for people who need a warm (or cool) place to rest. But agreeing in theory and expressing the opinion over a hearty lunch is different than rubbing shoulders and sharing hymnals. His sleeping felt a little rude.

The passing of the peace roused him, and he pulled a small blanket over his shoulders. As the offering plates made their way down the aisle, I ruffled through my wallet. A twenty-dollar bill and two ones. I made the mental calculations. I might need the twenty for a cab ride back to the hotel. I hate to be completely cashless. What if I needed to pick something up at the store? I quickly pulled the dollar bills and folded them so no one could see the denomination. The homeless man reached into his pocket and withdrew several coins. When the plate passed, I put in two dollars. He gave the entire handful.

I have never felt so naked. I, who have much, gave little. And he, the modern-day widow of the gospels, gave his last coins in service to God. I longed for one of his blankets, dirty and torn, to cover my shame.

—RICHELLE THOMPSON

Clothing collection boxes seem to be everywhere these days. It takes little effort to clean out a closet or bureau, throw your old clothes in a bag, and take them to the nearest box. The process makes us feel good. We get rid of unwanted clothing, make room for new additions to our own wardrobes, and someone gets our hand-me-downs.

Our church is the recipient of a great deal of clothing from well-meaning donors. Some of the clothing really does help cover the bodies of our friends. But much of what we receive gets thrown away. Sweaters covered in matted dog hair, coats with broken zippers, stained shirts. And we hear the excuse, "If somebody is cold, isn't this better than nothing?"

Well, to a point maybe, but as Christians we are as much about handing out dignity as we are about handing out clothes, aren't we? We often use the rule of thumb: "If you wouldn't give it to Jesus to wear, don't give it to one of your brothers or sisters in Christ." For our brothers and sisters *are* Jesus.

The issue of giving our cast-offs to those who have less is, at its heart, a question of stewardship. We can choose to give out of our overabundance what we no longer need or want, or we can choose to look at the bigger picture and ask ourselves what "the least of these" really need. In the end, the answer is the same for all of us—we need self-worth, dignity, and satisfaction in our accomplishments.

How we relate to others and how we manage our relative wealth are fundamental questions of faith. What might you have that someone else really needs? Can you give time to tutor children or adults so that they will be prepared for jobs that pay enough to buy clothing? Are you in a position to hire workers? Will you vote with the interests of *all* people in mind?

Truly I tell you, just as you did it to one of the least of these who are members of my family, you did it to me.

—LEE ANNE REAT

MARCH 11

"I don't know" is the most difficult thing for me to say out loud. Likewise, it is the most frightening condition I can find myself in. This fear has been one of the constants, along with other masks I've worn to cover up the vulnerability—the nakedness—that is at my core.

The first time I remember this condition was in fourth grade. We'd just moved to Oklahoma from a Shoshone reservation in Wyoming. Some forty years later I still remember the pit in my stomach as I looked down at my new desk and realized I didn't know how it operated. In my old school, the desks were a different design, and I couldn't figure the new one out.

I forced myself to look up as I held my books and school equipment in my lap. My fears were confirmed; everyone was looking at me. "Hey, dude, you can put your books there." The friendly face and guidance of the guy who would someday be our quarterback and pitcher should have put me at ease. But it didn't. You see, my "dis-ease" is an internal condition and nothing outside was ever and is ever going to be the solution.

New friendships didn't make me feel less different or less naked. Neither did using drugs and alcohol. Same with overachieving and people pleasing. Overeating and other overcompensations didn't do the trick either.

Finally, one day, broke and vulnerable in myriad ways—naked—I finally managed to take off the masks and acknowledge my condition and speak it out loud. What I found in that acknowledgment and acceptance was the presence of God and the solution to my dis-ease. I discovered another thing: when I shared my brokenness and vulnerability with others, it helped them to do the same. And in those moments, I was doing exactly what I was created to do and being exactly who I was created to be.

To be human is to be naked. Jesus understands that.

—**Bo Cox**

And the man and his wife were both naked, and were not ashamed....
And the LORD God made garments of skins for the man and for his
wife, and clothed them. —Genesis 2:25, 3:21

Jesus says that when we clothe the naked, we are clothing him.
And so we are.

His words harken back to the first clothing of the naked
in Eden. It is an act of sorrowful compassion by a God whose
dreams for humanity have been dashed. They have betrayed and
disappointed God, given God every reason to abandon them or
smite them out of wrath. And yet God cares for them...even as
we are called to care for one another as images of God.

But there is an even deeper truth, one that Jesus invites us
to confront: we are not made for clothes. Genesis tells us that
clothes are a concession. Before the fall, when God was at the
center and all was well, we were naked and unashamed. After
the fall, without God at the center of our lives, we are afraid and
naked, and we hide ourselves.

Jesus bids us to clothe the naked, and when we do so, we
know we are loving him, because that is what compassion looks
like. But the deeper truth is that we are not made for clothes.
We are made to be just as we are—and to be that way without
shame. We are made to rejoice in our own creation in God's
image, to not let our joy be quenched, and never to hide any part
of ourselves in fear of how someone else might view us.

So yes, let us clothe the naked. And in doing so, let us know we are serving Jesus. But let's remember that God's ultimate dream for us is not to need clothes. To rejoice that we are beautifully made, to be naked and unashamed.

—MIKE KINMAN

CHAPTER 5

Meditations on Matthew 25

*I was sick and you
took care of me*

For eighteen years, St. Augustine's Chapel has sent a group to San Eduardo, Ecuador. A centerpiece of this pilgrimage is the three-day medical clinic in that village that sees more than 900 patients annually. Every year we take pills, ointments, and liquids. But one year the doctor who directed the clinic reminded me that the most important healing we did was touching—a touch that communicates kindness and opens a space for healing to begin. The healing touch permeates all time and cultures. Shaman, rabbis, and ministers lay on hands to those suffering. And those suffering expose the weakest or most painful part of themselves to receive the gift.

When many people think about taking care of the sick, doctors and nurses come to mind, as do other professionals among us whose vocational calling is healing and curing. But the calling to take care of the sick is for all of us. Those who were hearing Jesus' words lived in a world where sickness could provoke an inquiry about the life of sin that had caused the unhealthy condition. Those who were afflicted could find themselves isolated, shunted aside, pushed to the fringes of the community. Those bearing diseases and disabilities were in need of care beyond the treatment of their physical maladies.

And so it is today. Matthew's Gospel is a call to bring healing through touch and words to those who suffer. Jesus reminds us that healing is not a commodity one person offers another but a grace that washes over all of us. We are called to take care of each other when we are sick. We heal one another when we have been stigmatized or socially marginalized and someone offers us a kind word or a loving touch. That kind of healing does not belong to doctors and nurses alone. We don't have the miraculous healing touch that Jesus had, yet we can work to restore our community so that when we are down and out, we are brought up and in, which can be a miracle of its own.

—BECCA STEVENS

March 14

The eyes do a good many things, a good many more than their biology would dictate.

Eyes pierce.

Eyes behold.

Eyes glitter, shine, and smile.

Eyes have borne witness and absorbed pain and promise.

Eyes stand sentinel and form the boundary between soul and space. They perceive and absorb the pathos and power of lived stories, catching, collecting, and storing up pericopes in the crevices of the soul.

They absorb so much that words fail to describe what the eyes have seen.

The immensity of all that our eyes have seen weighs heavy. The scenes leave us wordless, mute, often dumb. They bring joy as we entertain our loveliest memories. They devastate as they invade our nightmares.

It is said, "Do not judge a man until you have walked a mile in his shoes."

I say, "Do not judge a people until you have seen with their eyes, their world-wearied, heavy, too-tired eyes."

The eyes are the window into our souls; they are the prism that colors our world.

A sickness may lurk behind those eyes—not a sickness of body or even of mind, but a malady of the soul. A hole in the fabric of the psyche, a rupture in the self.

The scenes of life have generated a number of seeds that have been planted in the soil of our souls. What have our souls cultivated?

Seeds of loss, seeds of grief.

Seeds of devastation, seeds of trouble.

Seeds of sorrow and seeds of injustice.

What sickness may be growing behind those eyes?

And what small kindness, what small prayers, what small gestures of compassion and love—to a stranger on the street, to a neighbor struggling with loss, to a student at your local elementary school—can your soul share?

What scenes of grace and generosity, of patience and care can plant new seeds in the soil of another's soul?

In your words and deeds, even in the smallest of gestures, you can pepper the soul soil with antibodies of grace.

Your presence, your kindness, your love—these are the seeds that, once planted, can crowd out the cancerous growth hiding behind pained eyes.

—**ALLISON DUVALL**

March 15

She comes to Street Church often, standing outside the circle murmuring to herself, not making eye contact, fearful of touch. He shows up wearing colorful scarves or a colander on his head, carrying sticks or metal rods or stuffed animals. Many are drug and/or alcohol addicted.

Several are on crutches or in wheelchairs. Some are just exhausted from life on the streets.

She comes to Street Church in designer jeans wearing a big smile as she greets others, but her heart is broken by the recent death of her partner. He drives up in an expensive car, sporting a new leather jacket. He has struggled for years with alcohol addiction. Many are longing for meaning in life. Several have well-hidden but festering wounds. Some are exhausted from life in the fast lane.

Sickness of mind, body, or spirit is a great equalizer. We all break at some point. And we are all in need of healing. Whether at Street Church or in a cathedral, we come together in our brokenness to be touched by the healing power of God, to share the Body and Blood of Christ and to experience the care and concern of others.

Christ calls us to care for the sick. We do this every time we come together in worship. Our liturgy moves us through our need for healing to the assurance of wholeness. We begin worship by opening our hearts to God as we pray and hear the challenge and comfort of God's Word in scripture and proclamation. We pray for our needs and for the needs of others, then confess our brokenness to God. As we hear the words of absolution spoken and pass the Peace to those around us, we experience a turning point in the liturgy. Our sins are forgiven, hope is restored, and we once again prepare to gather at the table with our sisters and brothers in Christ to savor the richness of the heavenly banquet. Christ's body broken for us. We are cared for in our sickness, healed, and sent out to love and serve the Lord.

—LEE ANNE REAT

March 16

Bill Stone was a good man. When my wife moved to Oklahoma from Kentucky, Bill and his sister hired Debb. Even though she soon felt at home with them, she was afraid to tell them about me—her boyfriend serving time for murder. It turned out not to matter; Bill was as forgiving and accepting as a person could be.

Bill was a retired colonel in the Army. After retirement from the military, he went back to school, became a certified public accountant, and started doing business with some local hardware stores. When I got out of prison, he offered me a job. He sat me down and let me know that he would do anything he could to help me continue the success I'd started building while I was incarcerated. While I went another direction job-wise, I often stopped in Bill Stone's office for advice and for pep talks.

We were as different as two people could be, yet he never failed to let me know that he supported me and even admired me. Many times I'd drop my head and look at my feet when he told me how admirable my journey was and what strength he drew from me.

And so when Bill started to suffer from Parkinson's disease, I vowed to try and be there for him like he'd been there for me. At first, it seemed like he'd conquer it. He continued to drive and work—even continued golfing—all while the disease began to literally fold him in half. For a while, I kept my vow; I'd stop in regularly to offer some cheer. (Of course, he'd inevitably end up cheering me up.)

Meeting Jesus on the Margins

Toward the end, I let my fear and discomfort keep me from going to see him, and when he died I became well-acquainted with the regret that is still with me to this day. However, the nature of my regret has changed. I didn't let Bill down; I let myself down. What I've come to know is that I needed to go see Bill for me, not for him.

—Bo Cox

Intermittently hot and then shaking with chills, aching throughout my body, I was more than sick; I was scared. My command of Arabic was weak; I had only been staying with my host family in Rabat, Morocco, for a few weeks. On top of that, it was the holy month of Ramadan, a sacred time. The daily fasts had my host parents and siblings tired and very hungry at the end of the day. The scent of lentil soup wafted from the tiny kitchen as all of Morocco prepared for the call to prayer announcing sundown and the end of the day's fast—the *ftour*.

My elder sister Fatima sat next to me, dabbing my forehead with a cool cloth, just as the calls began to ring out across the city. "You will be better," she said. My father came in the room, and he and Fatima spoke rapidly in Arabic. "We will take you to the doctor," Fati said. "Oui, doctor," said my father.

Their *ftour* would wait. They supported me as we slowly walked out of the apartment and into the street to hail a taxi. For many hours into the night, long after the breaking of the fast, they stayed with me. Fati held my hand as I cried softly, and she continued to cool my flushed skin with washcloths. My father, in French, assured me all would be well. He and Fati mediated between me and the doctor; I was too tired and bewildered to stumble through my mess of Arabic and French.

By the time we made it home and Fati helped me into bed, making sure I was comfortable, only a few hours remained before the sun would rise and the fast would begin again. My father came to the door of the salon where I slept, looked in, and offered a sweet "Good night" in broken English. Fati placed a cool cloth on my forehead and joined him for a simple meal.

This memory has been my guiding light, my offering when I hear someone speak of Muslims with suspicion, mistrust, or prejudice. I tell them of the time I was very very sick and how my loving Muslim family cared for me. I think of Psalm 133: *Oh how good and pleasant it is when brethren live together in unity!* And I think, in gratitude, of how my sense of family and brethren expanded in relationship with my Moroccan family.

—ALLISON DUVALL

March 18

From the day I arrived in Paraguay as a missionary, I always carried with me, in a secret compartment, $150 of emergency money. It soon became apparent that I probably wouldn't need the money because all of my needs—food, rent, transportation, clothing—were taken care of by the church. Had I gotten sick, I would have gone to a clinic—with all expenses paid.

Shortly after arriving, I met Ramiro. He was a subsistence fisherman whose family lived in a shack, mere yards from the Paraguay River. Every morning, Ramiro climbed into his boat with a net and a fishing pole. Every evening, he fed his family, or sold whatever the river had provided.

One day I saw a bandage around Ramiro's leg. "I think I broke it," he said. "I can't walk or work." Twice, Ramiro consulted a local healer, but the healer's teas failed to cure him. I decided to blow my reserve money and take him to a clinic. That $150 covered his x-rays, the cast, and the follow-up visit to evaluate his progress and remove the cast. And I still had $20 left in my wallet!

I was only twenty-two years old when I went on that mission. Looking back, I feel embarrassed about many things I did in my younger days. But not about spending that emergency money. I remember with gratitude the day Ramiro was able to get back on his boat and continue to provide for his family.

—Hugo Olaiz

MARCH 19

Flesh-eating bacteria. Have to cut until it's gone. Critical condition.

The doctor's words arrived in my head but jumbled around, almost nonsensical. Down the corridor, my thirty-five-year-old husband lay in intensive care, covered in sweat but shaking with cold. I sank to the chair in the family waiting area. At a new church in a new city, our support network was nascent. I called a friend and then the deacon of the congregation. At 9 p.m., we were allowed into the ICU for ten minutes. I leaned down to kiss his forehead, and his eyes fluttered. But in his delirium, I'm not sure he knew who I was. I held his hand and held back tears as the deacon said the words of Compline.

The Lord Almighty grant us a peaceful night and a perfect end. Amen.

Our help is in the Name of the Lord;
The maker of heaven and earth.

I looked up. The words fell out of his mouth. Mumbled but coherent. He began to pray with us.

Almighty God, our heavenly Father…

As the prayer ended, the tears flowed freely. The tests showed later that he didn't have the flesh-eating bacteria—necrotizing fasciitis—but a wicked infection. He still spent two more weeks in the hospital and came home with an IV for another long round of antibiotics. But he was home and, eventually, well.

I was sick and you took care of me

I met Jesus that night in the liturgy, as it provided words when my husband couldn't form his own. It gave him structure and form so he could offer prayers of petition, contrition, and thanksgiving when sickness took everything else.

When we comfort the sick, we meet Jesus, and we meet him again when he comforts us right back, embracing the hurting and the worried alike. Thanks be to God.

—RICHELLE THOMPSON

CHAPTER 6

Meditations on Matthew 25

I was in prison and you visited me

Palm Sunday

During the orientation for prison volunteers, they tell you the myriad ways you have to be on your guard against the people you are attempting to serve. Be careful, they say, or the prisoners will try to get your shoes, your phone number, your bank account numbers, your address, your wife; the list goes on, ad infinitum.

I've been in prison, and I know that, for the most part, people in prison are just that: people. I bristle when I encounter systems that are designed to further stigmatize and polarize members of the same race—that is, the human race.

Despite the fact that the prisons of Jesus' day and the prisons of our day barely resemble one another, Jesus knew that the second we deny the humanity and sacredness in the most marginalized, we begin to close a spiritual door in ourselves and, eventually, lose our own connection to the Light.

I doubt it was to put a capital P in Pious that Jesus urged us to visit those in prison. And while it may be that your visit could brighten someone else's day and possibly even change his or her life for the better, I don't think that was the reason for his admonition.

Jesus knew that to the extent we are unable to see and trust the sacred goodness in the worst of us, we will likewise fail to see the brokenness in the best. Ultimately, we will lose our connection to our fellow humans and to God.

Go to prison. Look into the eyes of another and see yourself. And your God. That's what Jesus wanted for us.

—**Bo Cox**

March 21

In early October of 2014, I spent the day in jail.

I wasn't an inmate. I was there because twelve young women and men had been arrested the night before, protesting in front of the police department in Ferguson, Missouri. The night before, I had been standing with them as they protested how they and their sisters and brothers have been treated by police.

Video showed that in some cases, they were pushed off the sidewalk and then arrested for being in the street.

I was there with a group of about a dozen other clergy, and we weren't going to leave until these young people got out.

Not because we were their leaders…but because they were ours.

Jesus tells us to visit the prisoners, and that's where we'll find him. That command took on new meaning to me that day. If you're truly going to follow Jesus and try to be Jesus for the world, you've got a good chance of landing in jail. Just ask Martin Luther King Jr. or Gandhi (who revered the Sermon on the Mount) or Jesus himself.

As clergy we often think we visit prisoners to bring them Jesus, but Jesus is clear it's the other way around. I saw Jesus that day. Her name was Alexis Templeton. Her name was Brittany Ferrell. Her name was Ashley Yates.

I saw Jesus that day. Willing to lay down her life for the sake of making the world more just.

And Jesus looked at me and said:

"Where have you been? You've been sitting in your churches, and we're out here dying."

"You want to help? Face the tear gas and the pepper spray and the rubber bullets with us."

These days any number of people will tell you their opinions about how to grow the church. I have lost interest in all of them. Because just about all of the opinions are about how I can get people to come into my church.

Growing the church is not about getting people into my building. Growing the church is about being out in the streets… and sitting in jail cells.

That's where Jesus is.

—MIKE KINMAN

MARCH 22

There is nothing like the sound of the metal automatic doors closing behind you when you visit someone in prison. It is a stark reminder that our lives are not in our control and that the freedom we take for granted is a precious pearl in a prison field.

I have heard people say they are "taking Jesus" into the prison. In the twenty years or so that I have visited people inside those walls, my view is that if you want to feel the presence of Jesus, go to prison. People don't bring Jesus to prison. He is already there with the prisoners. You can see Jesus in the fear, longing, sickness, injustice, and gratitude of people you meet inside. I have known many women who knew the backside of anger, the underside of bridges, and the short side of justice long before they knew the inside of prison walls. If it was not for their undying faith that Jesus was walking through the system with them, they would not make it.

"I was in prison and you visited me." Those in prison are isolated, cut off from interaction in the community that nourishes all of us. Visitors are the prisoners' line to life, the life that was theirs and for some, the life that they hope will be theirs again. Even one visit can help to sustain their faith that Jesus can be found on that path and the hope that the community has not abandoned them.

Sometimes I dread having to go to prison. But as the doors open and I walk out and back into my life, I always feel a profound humility that I was near the Lord.

Meeting Jesus on the Margins

My Lord and my God, my prayers go out today to all the prisoners, their families, the guards, and especially the children of those incarcerated. You teach us to go to the prisons, to see the truth of your suffering, and then to leave more committed to tearing down those walls. Never let us forget where it is you reside. Amen.

—BECCA STEVENS

MARCH 23

Thirty years ago, a scared young man of twenty-three sat behind the glass in a secure visiting room, seeing the shocked look on his parents' faces as they got their first glimpse of their son as #150656, doing a life sentence. They were unable to control their fear; what they saw was more akin to a wild animal than the boy they'd raised well. He knew something was wrong by the look in their eyes, but he didn't realize he was the source.

Not only did he not possess the faculties to grasp the obvious fact that he was the reason for their pain, he also didn't and couldn't understand the horror of another set of parents—the parents of the young man he'd killed.

Not long after, returning from another visit with his parents, he was told by an old timer to wipe that grin off his face because, eventually, his parents would stop coming to see him. That was just the nature of the beast, the cynical convict said with a smirk.

Thankfully, the fortune-teller prisoner was wrong, and the parents never stopped coming to see the young man. They visited him through the remainder of his twenties and all but a few months of his thirties and continued to be pillars of consistency and support during the years it took to readjust to life on the outside.

In addition to his parents, a handful of prison volunteers came into his life and treated him like he was normal, even like he was part of their family.

In his case, the old cynical convict was wrong. However, there were also many souls in that dark place who failed to either get or make a positive and life-changing connection with someone who was on a good path.

Today, I am a man of fifty-two, who goes to visit prisoners, because I know what it was like to need a good example. And I know firsthand that no one is ever too lost to be found.

—Bo Cox

MARCH 24

Many of us read *The Scarlet Letter* in high school. Hester Prynne was forced to wear a large letter "A" as punishment for her sin—an outward and visible sign of what was judged to be an inward and spiritual disgrace.

Today we shutter at the thought of such public shaming, yet those who have served time in prison might just as well wear a large "F" for "Felon" as lifelong punishment for their criminal convictions. You see, ex-offenders, people who have served out their legal sentence in prison, are never actually set free. Years after imprisonment, years after release from parole, people who have paid their debt to society are still barred from many employment and housing opportunities.

Jack served sixteen years for a crime he committed as a young man. He struggles to find and keep employment, not because he isn't a hard worker but because of his felony conviction—even though his record has been clean for over twenty-five years. Janice was released from prison two years ago and has successfully completed a residential program for returning citizens. She cannot find anyone who will rent her an apartment, so she lives on the streets where her chances of falling back into addiction and crime are high.

We say that individuals are sentenced to a certain number of years. We say that the purpose of the prison system is rehabilitation. Yet discrimination based on past criminal convictions is widespread: once in prison, always in prison.

We may not have opportunities to visit prisoners while they are behind bars, though programs such as Kairos Prison Ministries afford us that possibility, but we can all impact what happens to returning citizens. Efforts are underway in cities and states to put an end to discrimination based on criminal background, unless the crime committed is directly related to the job in question. Talk to your city, county, and state representatives. Voice your concerns and vote your moral values. Jesus teaches us to love our enemies and to visit those in prison.

—LEE ANNE REAT

"The cross is safe. No lower to go."

My spiritual director, the Rev. Victoria Sirota, said these words to me, and they have shaped my life ever since.

There is no safer place in the world than the cross of Jesus Christ.

That's really hard to believe. How can the cross, of all places, be safe? The cross is a place of abandonment, of ridicule and shame, pain and despair. The cross is a place of death.

The cross of Jesus Christ is a place of everything we fear. It is a place of everything we spend our lives, time, energy, and money trying to flee from and protect ourselves against.

And that is why the cross is safe.

Because the cross of Jesus Christ is the only place where there is nothing left to fear. Where we have, in Paul's words, "counted all as lost" (Philipppians 3:8). There is no lower to go. And who is there is Christ. And in Christ's arms…well, in this world there is no safer place.

We have spent this Lent reflecting on Matthew 25. On meeting Christ in places of deep deprivation and loss. Good Friday tells us these are not day trips that end with us safely in our warm beds at night. Meeting Christ in the hungry, the thirsty, the naked, and the sick means we need to count everything as loss that separates ourselves from those people, knowing their arms are the arms of Christ.

Jesus said: "I was in prison and you visited me." Do we realize what he was saying to us? Jesus' prison was literally the cross…and those who visited him there risked being next. That's why most of them hid in fear.

Our last word of this Lent is nothing less than an invitation to the cross. Considering that invitation can be fearful beyond measure. So we must remind ourselves that as fearful as the cross is, the cross is safe, for there is no lower to go.

The cross is safe because Jesus is there.

—MIKE KINMAN

MARCH 26

In June 2009, while I was serving a Latino congregation in Durham, North Carolina, the senior warden phoned to tell me that the police had just arrested José, one of our musicians. Every Sunday morning, José used to be in church, in the first row, singing and playing the guitar.

I visited José at the county jail. We weren't allowed to meet face-to-face, not even through glass; we spoke via closed-circuit television. He told me that when the police stopped and searched his car, they found a Social Security number that wasn't his. They accused him of identity theft. "I didn't steal anyone's identity," José told me. "I invented that number!"

I knew that José had broken the law when he entered the US without a visa. I also knew that with his arrest, his company had lost a reliable worker; his family had lost a dear uncle; and at church, we had lost a brother.

The Sunday after his arrest, during Holy Eucharist, I asked the vestry to come up front, hold hands with me, and pray for José. We prayed that he would be protected while in jail, protected while dealing with a legal system he didn't understand, and protected all the way back to his native El Salvador. We knew he would be deported. We knew we would never see him again.

After the service, I went to the altar of the Virgin of Guadalupe, which stands just five feet away from the pew where José used to sit. Among the candles, flowers, and rosaries, I left there a photo of José.

—Hugo Olaiz

Easter

The homeless guy sat at our kitchen table with our daughter. Together they spooned deviled egg mix into the white halves. All of his clothes swished around in one load of the washing machine. My parents, newly separated but making the three-hour trip together, set the dining room table. A couple, two men together for more than twenty years, brought dessert. A young family pushed their son and ours on the swings in the yard.

Never before and never since has our dinner table been such a glorious representation of the kingdom of God. All too often the people we invite into our homes look like us, act like us, smell like us.

Perhaps it is no coincidence that this dinner was on Easter Sunday. We had only planned for our family and one of the couples. But after the worship service, we talked with a young family who had nowhere to go and with Joe, the homeless man, who had a solo date at the laundromat. Spontaneously we asked them to join us.

At the table, we took turns sharing our favorite Easter memories. Bonnets and bunnies, egg hunts and sunrise services, until it was time for Joe. Not many chocolate rabbits were delivered at the orphanage.

"This Easter," he said, "might be one of my favorites."

Friends, we have spent our Lent together, exploring how we might live into Jesus' call to feed the hungry, greet the stranger, care for the sick. We have examined our own thirsts, our naked vulnerabilities, our prisons. We have, as our Ash Wednesday meditation encouraged, engaged in "profound, grace-filled unburdening." But this time of reflection and introspection is the foundation for action. Jesus didn't rise from the dead to only sit at the right hand of God.

He conquered death, he came out of the empty tomb to walk with us, to teach us, and to urge us to help others, to be companions on the journey, and to see and celebrate the living Christ in all.

May your table—and your life—be a living witness and foretaste of the heavenly banquet.

Alleluia. Alleluia.

—RICHELLE THOMPSON

About the Authors

Bo Cox spends his time working at a state-run psychiatric hospital where he helps lead recreational activities and is a therapy dog handler. When he's not there, he's in the woods with his wife, Debb, and their furry children. Sometimes he finds time to write; he's written for Forward Movement for almost a quarter century; the first half of that from inside prison and the second half from outside. He prefers outside.

pages 22, 38, 46, 74, 86, 94, 100

Allison Duvall is a young adult hailing from the Diocese of Lexington. She has served as a parish musician at St. John's Episcopal Church in Versailles, Kentucky, and as the executive director of Reading Camp, a literacy ministry of the Diocese of Lexington for elementary-school students who are behind grade level in reading and other academic skills. In 2013, she joined the staff of Episcopal Migration Ministries (EMM), the refugee resettlement service of the Domestic and Foreign Missionary Society, as the manager for church relations and engagement. In this role, she supports the community outreach staff of thirty EMM local affiliate offices across the United States, and educates and equips dioceses, congregations, and individual Episcopalians to find their own place in the welcoming ministry of refugee resettlement. She served as a deputy to General Convention in

2009 and 2012 and currently serves as an at-large board member for Episcopal Appalachian Ministries.

pages 16, 25, 36, 44, 54, 64, 82, 88

MIKE KINMAN is the dean of Christ Church Cathedral, a vibrant Christian community and sacred public space in St. Louis—a place where all downtown comes together for celebration, conversation, and to work for the common good. His passion for the gospel is as a force for reconciliation, and in St. Louis that means the cathedral being in the middle of the deep divides of race and class. He serves as founding board president for Magdalene St. Louis, an organization modeled after the successful Magdalene program in Nashville that offers housing, supportive community, and a new life for women who have survived prostitution, abuse, addiction, and sex trafficking. Michael lives with his wife, Robin, and sons Schroedter and Hayden in St. Louis City.

pages 10, 50, 56, 60, 76, 96, 104

HUGO OLAIZ works for Forward Movement as the associate editor for Latino/Hispanic resources. Hugo was born in Argentina, where he spent half of his life. Always curious about foreign languages and cultures, he studied classics, linguistics, and translation in college. He serves as a greeter at Church of Our Savior, a bilingual parish (English and Spanish) in Mount Auburn, a historic neighborhood of Cincinnati. He lives in

Oxford, Ohio, with his husband, John-Charles, and an aging beagle-mix named Patches.

pages 14, 24, 34, 48, 68, 90, 106

LEE ANNE REAT is vicar at St. John's, Columbus, and coordinator of the Diocese of Southern Ohio's School for Diaconal Formation. St. John's serves a primarily Appalachian neighborhood and is home to Street Church (Holy Eucharist every Sunday on a street corner welcoming those who may not feel comfortable inside a church building), the Growing Place (an outdoor learning environment and worship space for the community), and Confluence (an Episcopal Service Corps program for young adults). Lee Anne holds degrees in theology, adult education, early childhood education, and public policy.

pages 12, 20, 32, 58, 72, 84, 102

BECCA STEVENS is a premier preacher and speaker in the United States, proclaiming love as the most powerful force for social change. She is an Episcopal priest and founder of Magdalene, residential communities of women who have survived prostitution, trafficking, and addiction. In 2001, Becca founded Thistle Farms, which currently employs sixty residents and program graduates, and houses a natural body care line, a paper and sewing studio, and the Thistle Stop Café. Her most recent book is *The Way of Tea and Justice: Rescuing the World's Favorite Beverage from its Violent History.*

pages 18, 28, 52, 66, 80, 98

RICHELLE THOMPSON serves as deputy director and managing editor at Forward Movement. Her passion for hearing and telling stories and writing in a way that moves people has guided her vocation, first as a newspaper reporter, then as director of communications for the Diocese of Southern Ohio, and continuing with her ministry at Forward Movement. She and her husband, an Episcopal priest, have two children, a horse, a dog, and two rabbits. They all live in God's country in Northern Kentucky.

pages 30, 40, 70, 91, 108

ABOUT FORWARD MOVEMENT

Forward Movement is committed to inspiring disciples and empowering evangelists. While we produce great resources like this book, Forward Movement is not a publishing company. We are a ministry.

Our mission is to support you in your spiritual journey, to help you grow as a follower of Jesus Christ. Publishing books, daily reflections, studies for small groups, and online resources is an important way that we live out this ministry. More than a half million people read our daily devotions through *Forward Day by Day,* which is also available in Spanish (*Adelante Día a Día*) and Braille, online, as a podcast, and as an app for your smartphones or tablets. It is mailed to more than fifty countries, and we donate nearly 30,000 copies each quarter to prisons, hospitals, and nursing homes. We actively seek partners across the Church and look for ways to provide resources that inspire and challenge.

A ministry of The Episcopal Church for eighty years, Forward Movement is a nonprofit organization funded by sales of resources and gifts from generous donors. To learn more about Forward Movement and our resources, please visit us at www.forwardmovement.org (or www.adelanteenelcamino.org).

We are delighted to be doing this work and invite your prayers and support.